# THIS BOOK

## BELONG TO



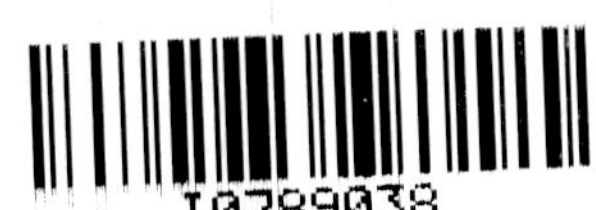

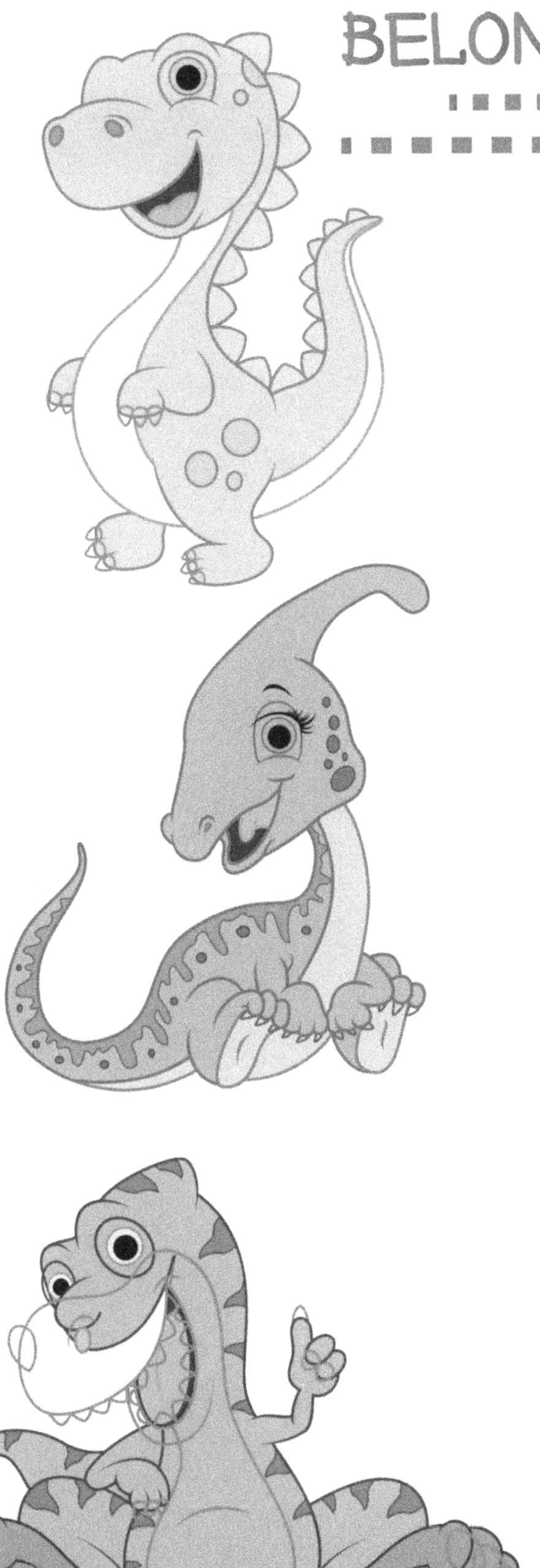

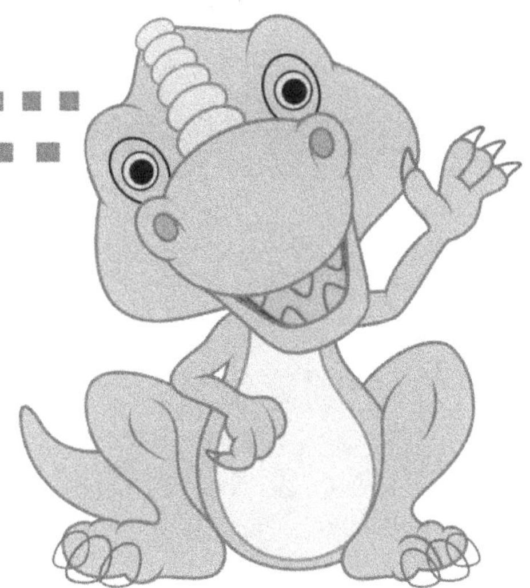

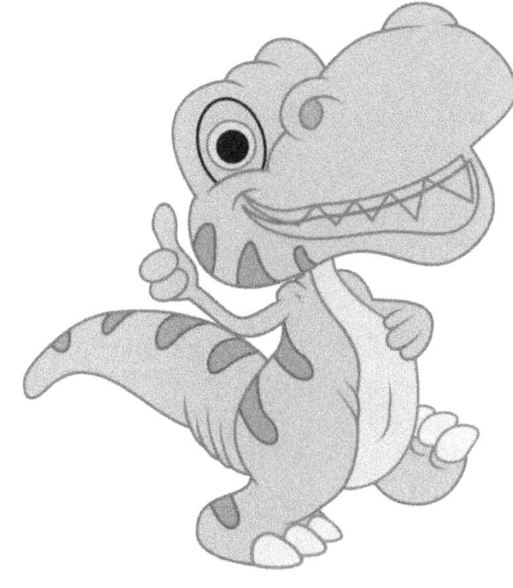

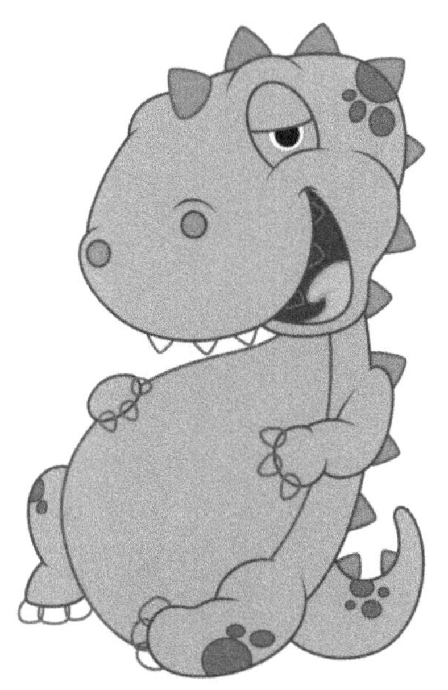

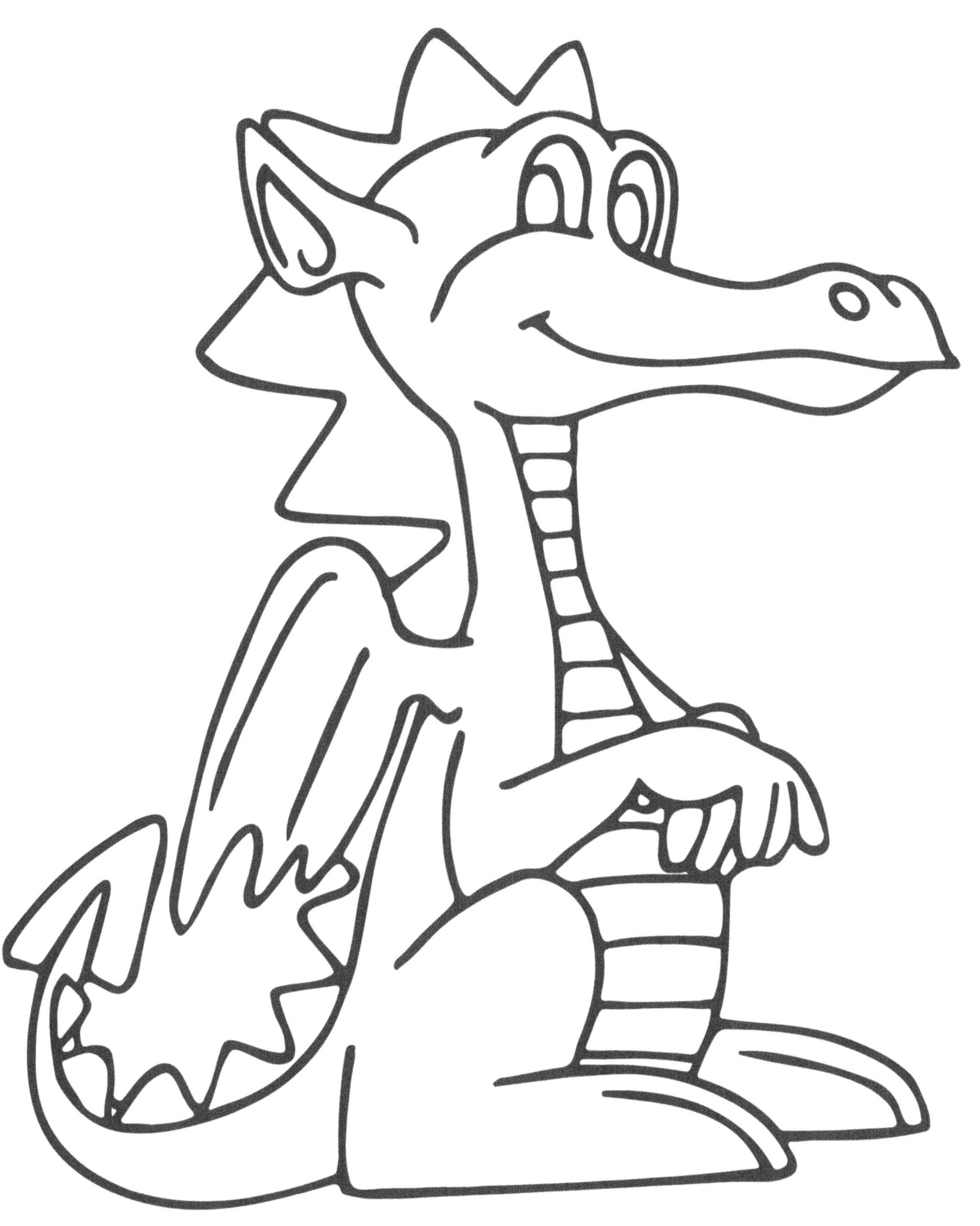

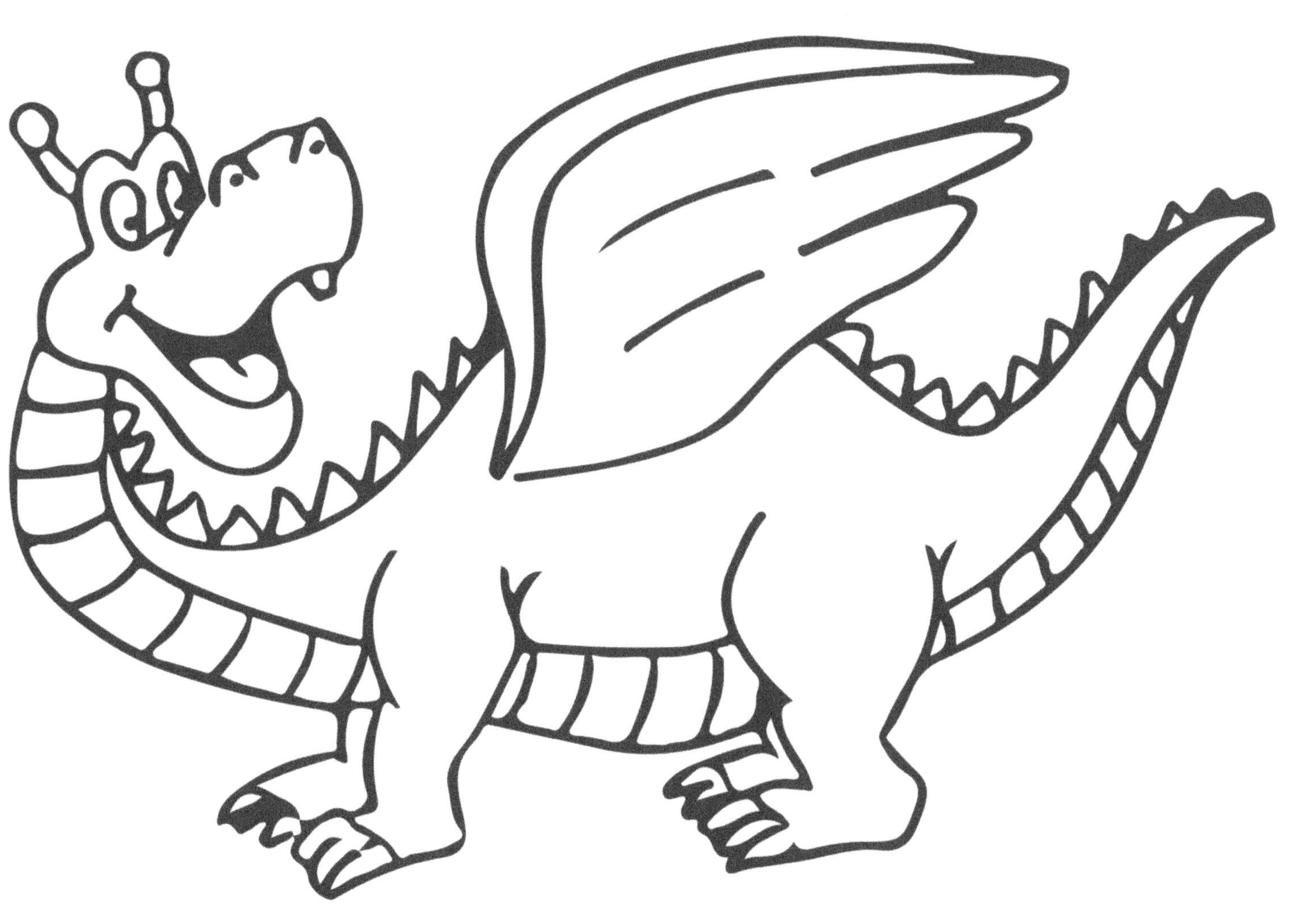

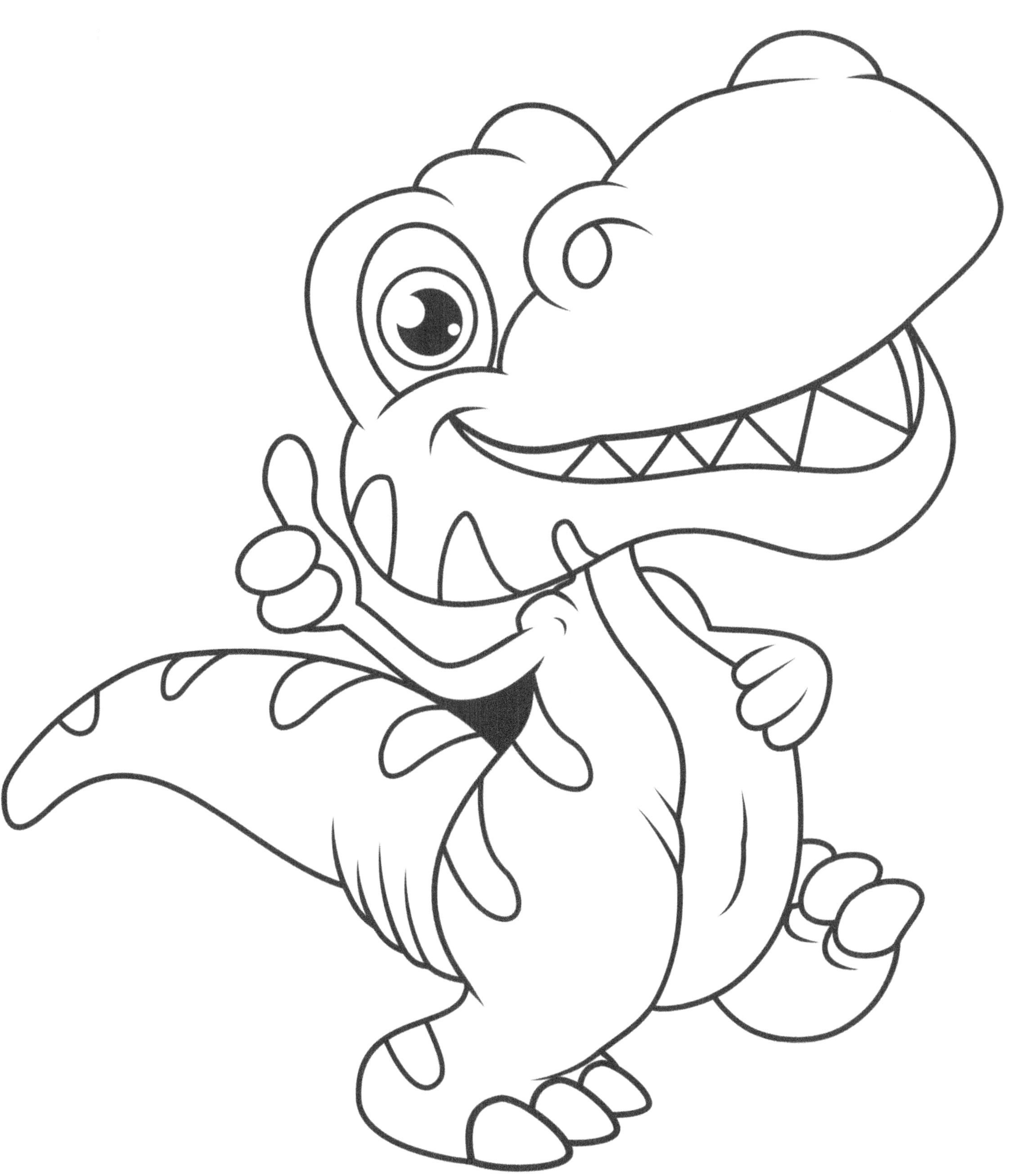

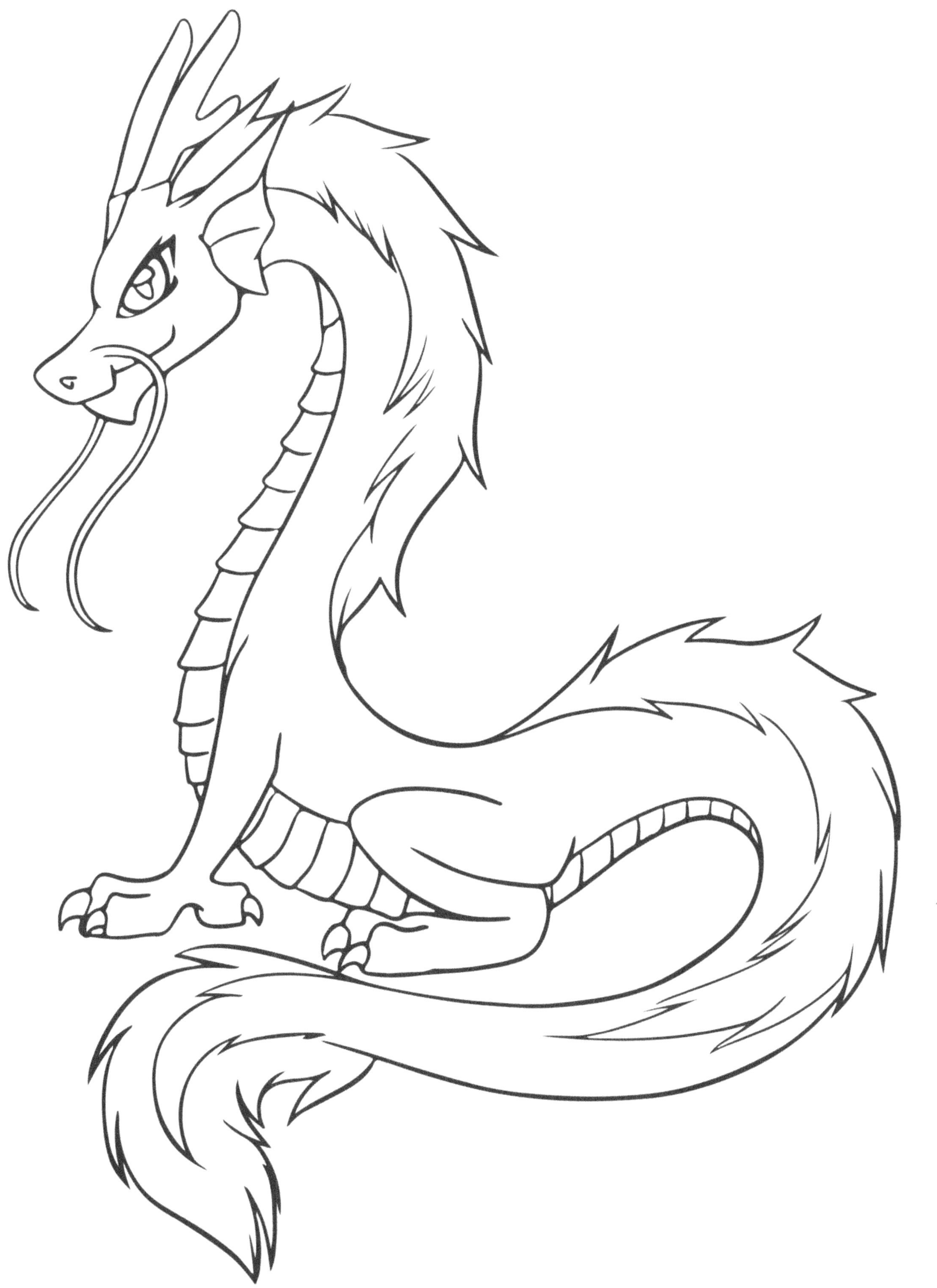

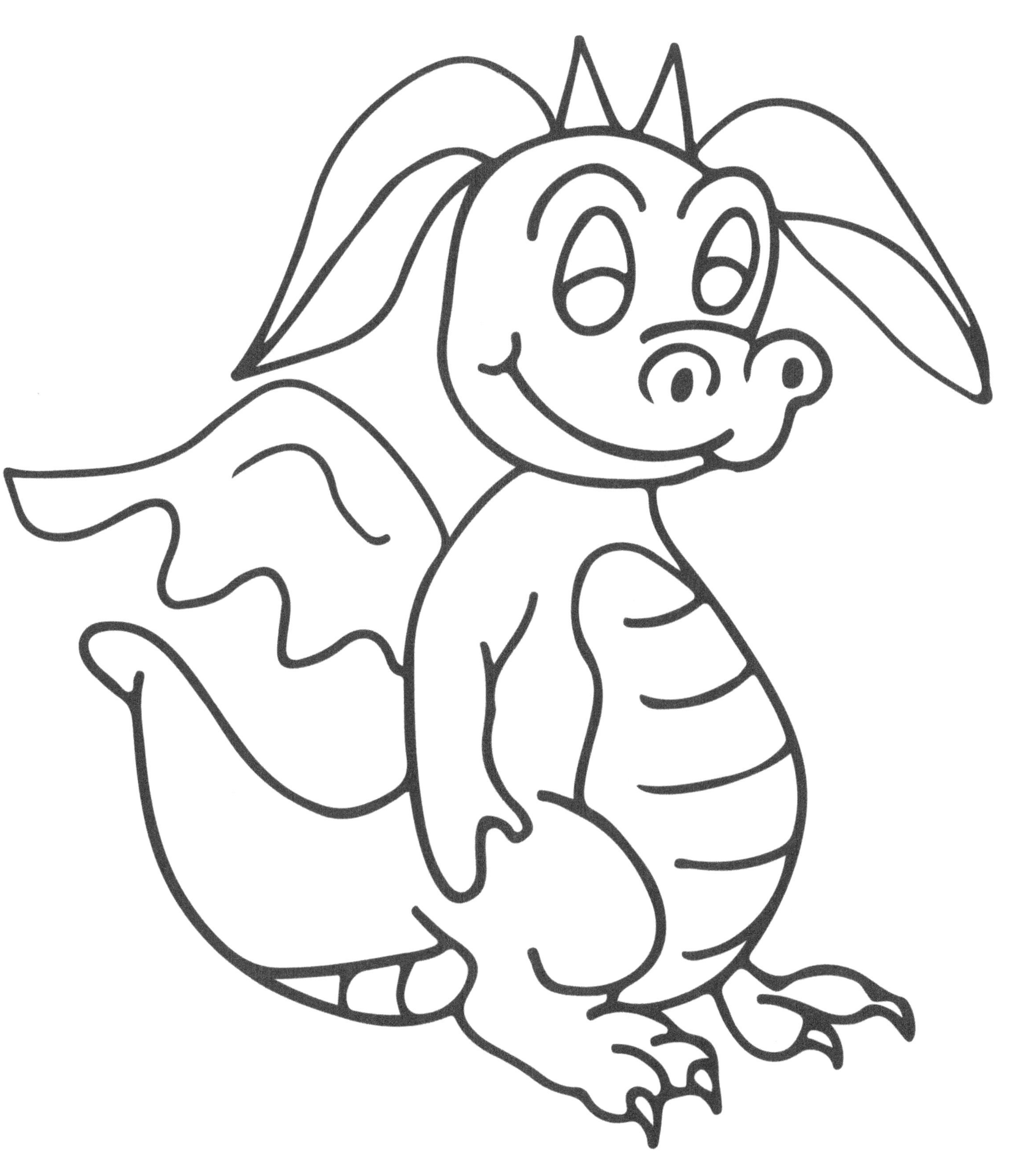

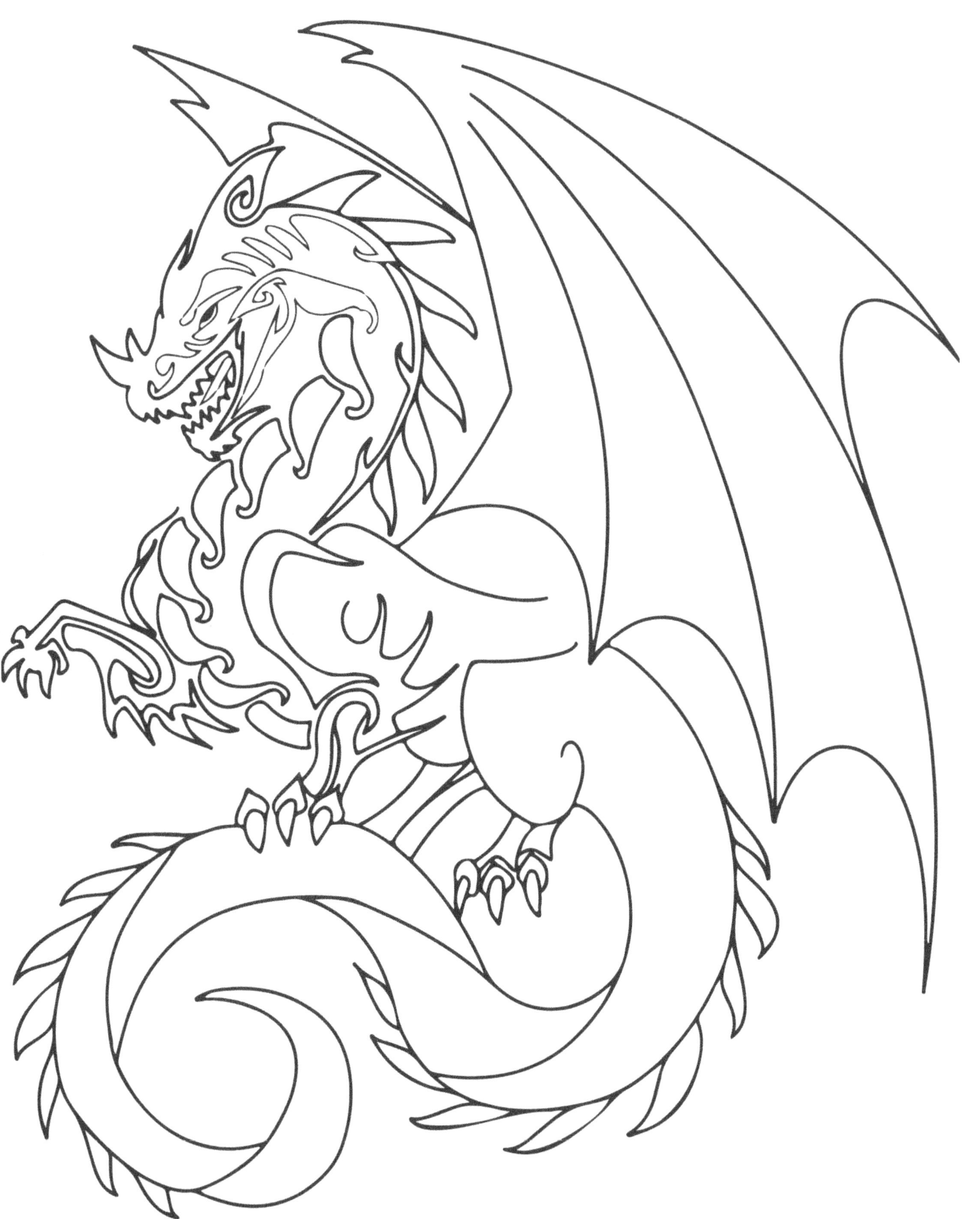

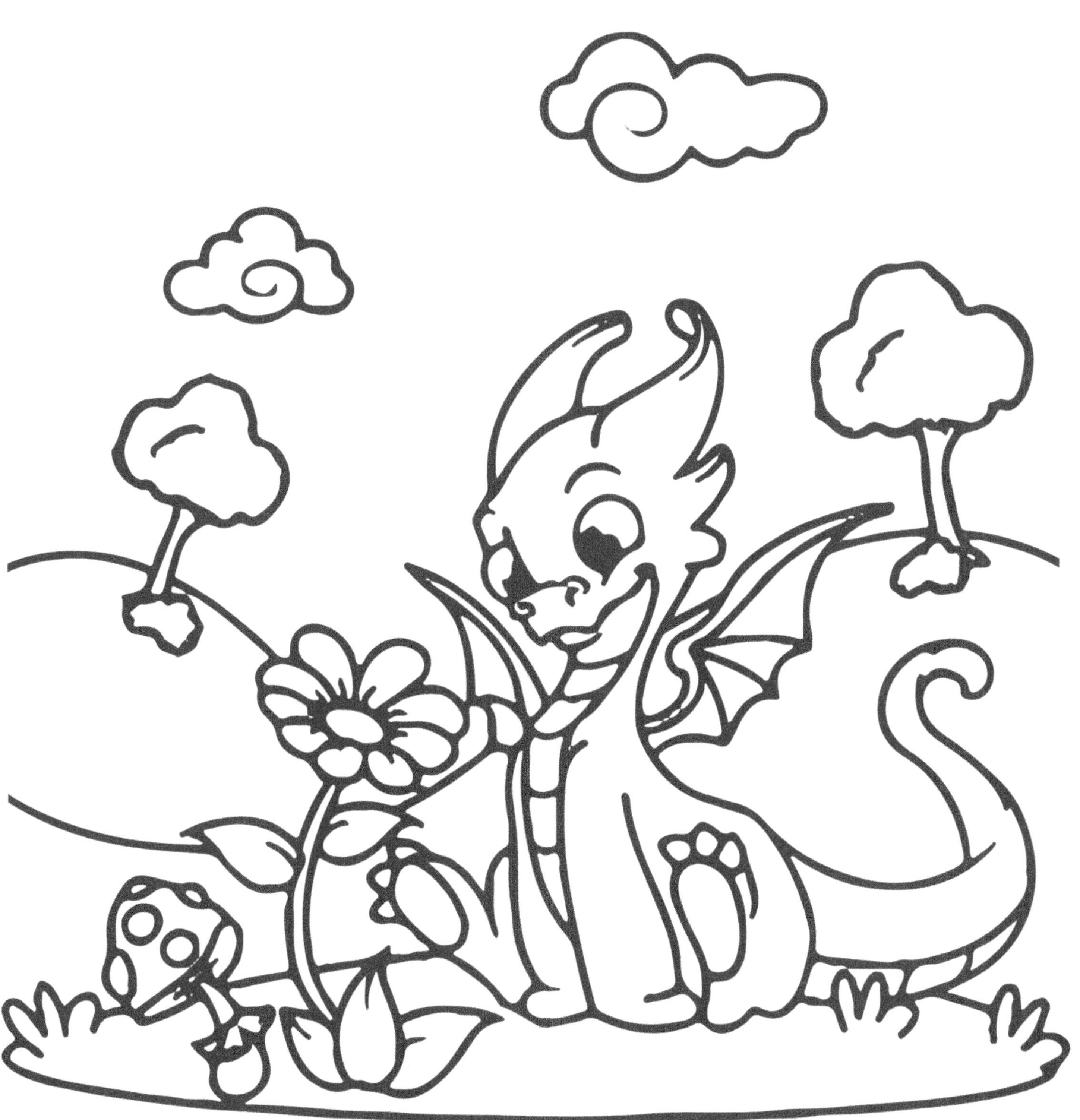

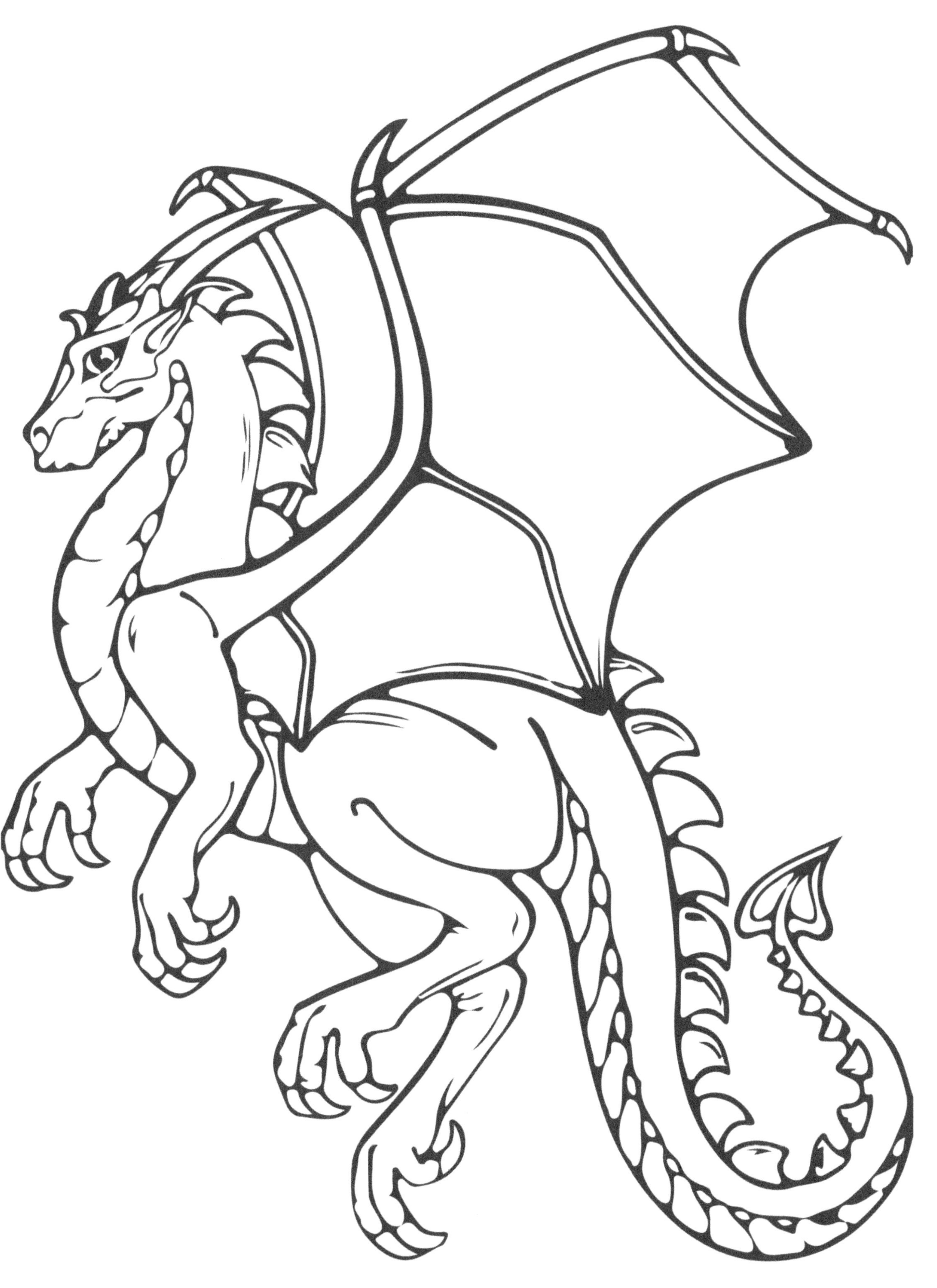

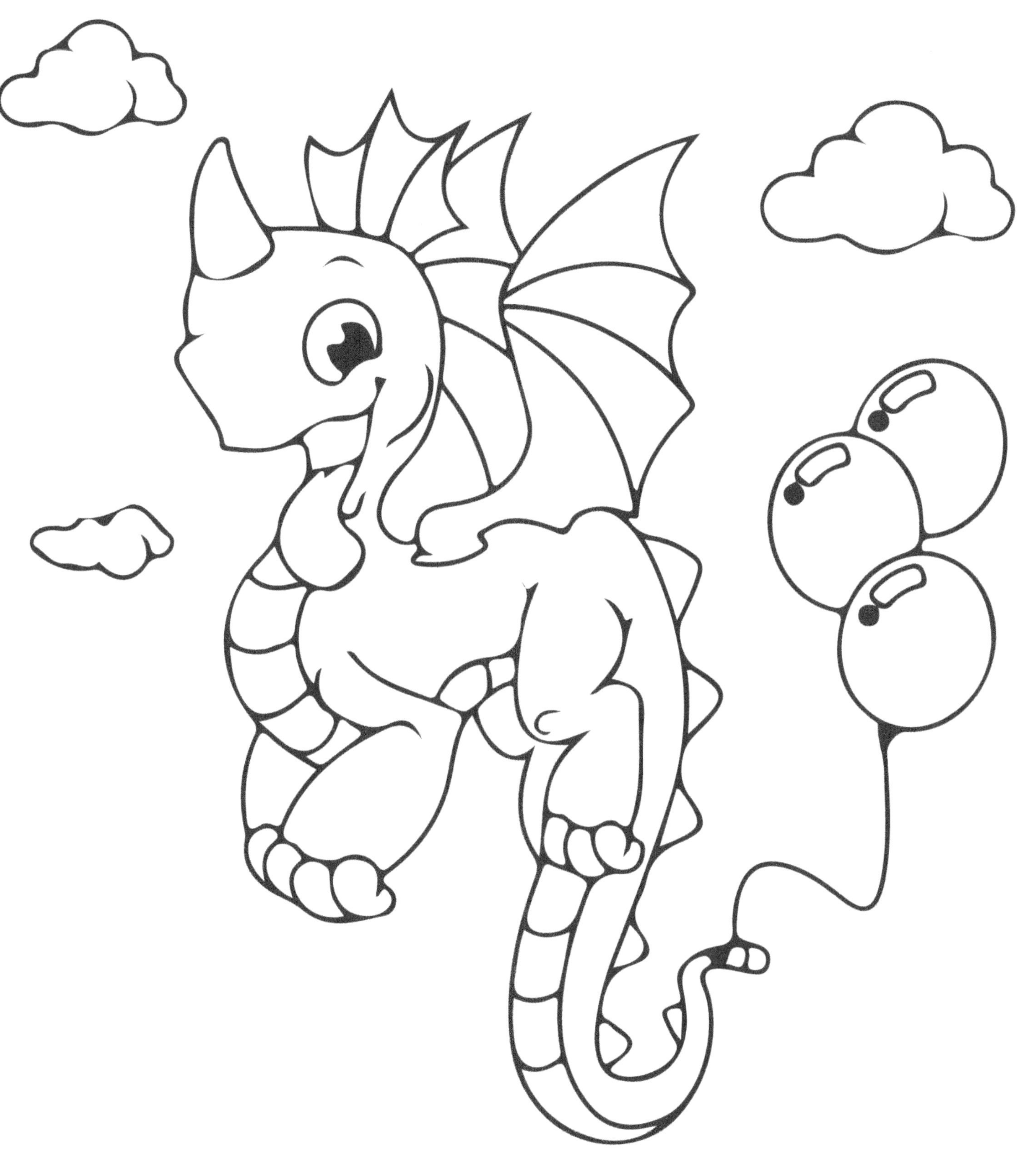

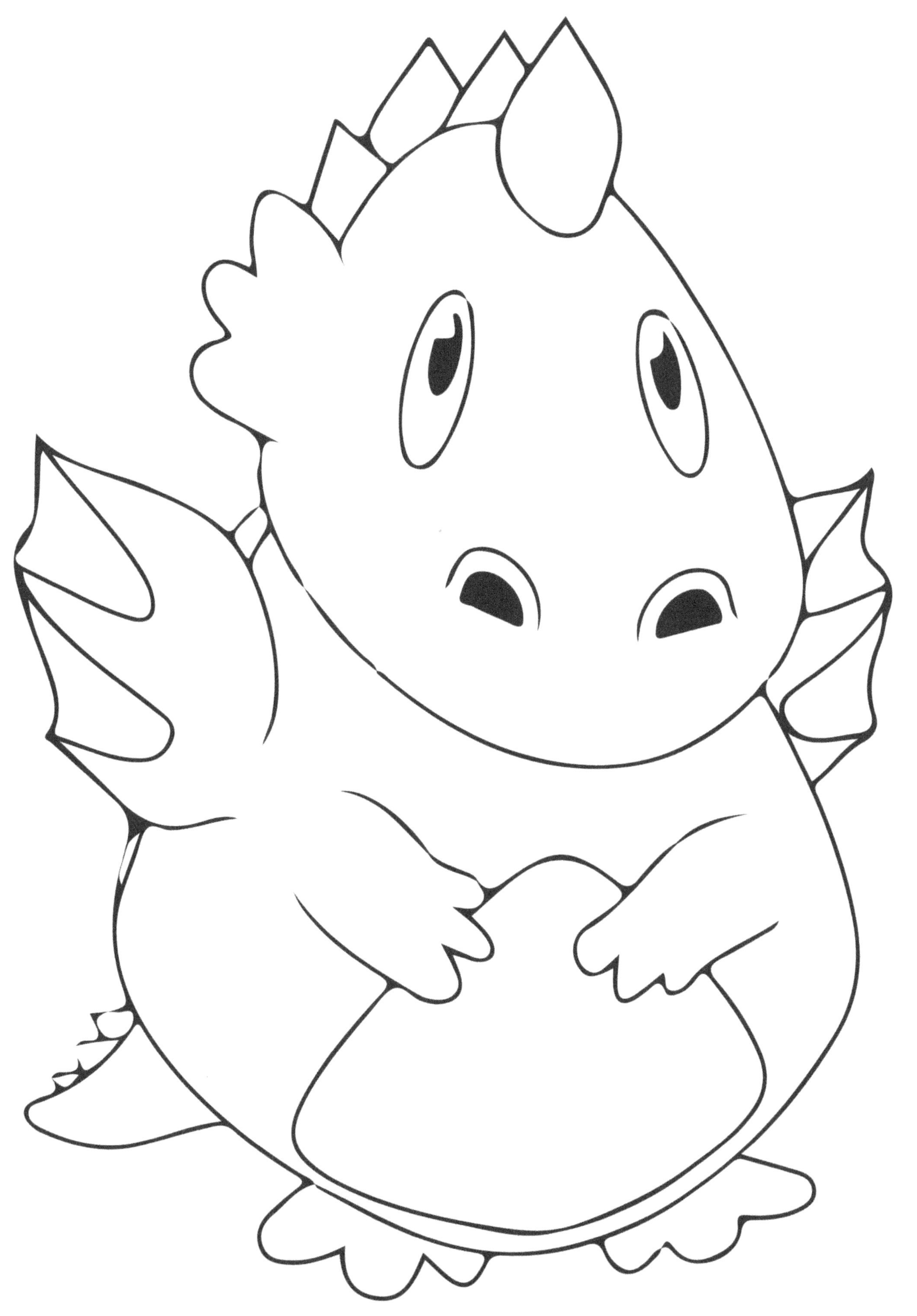

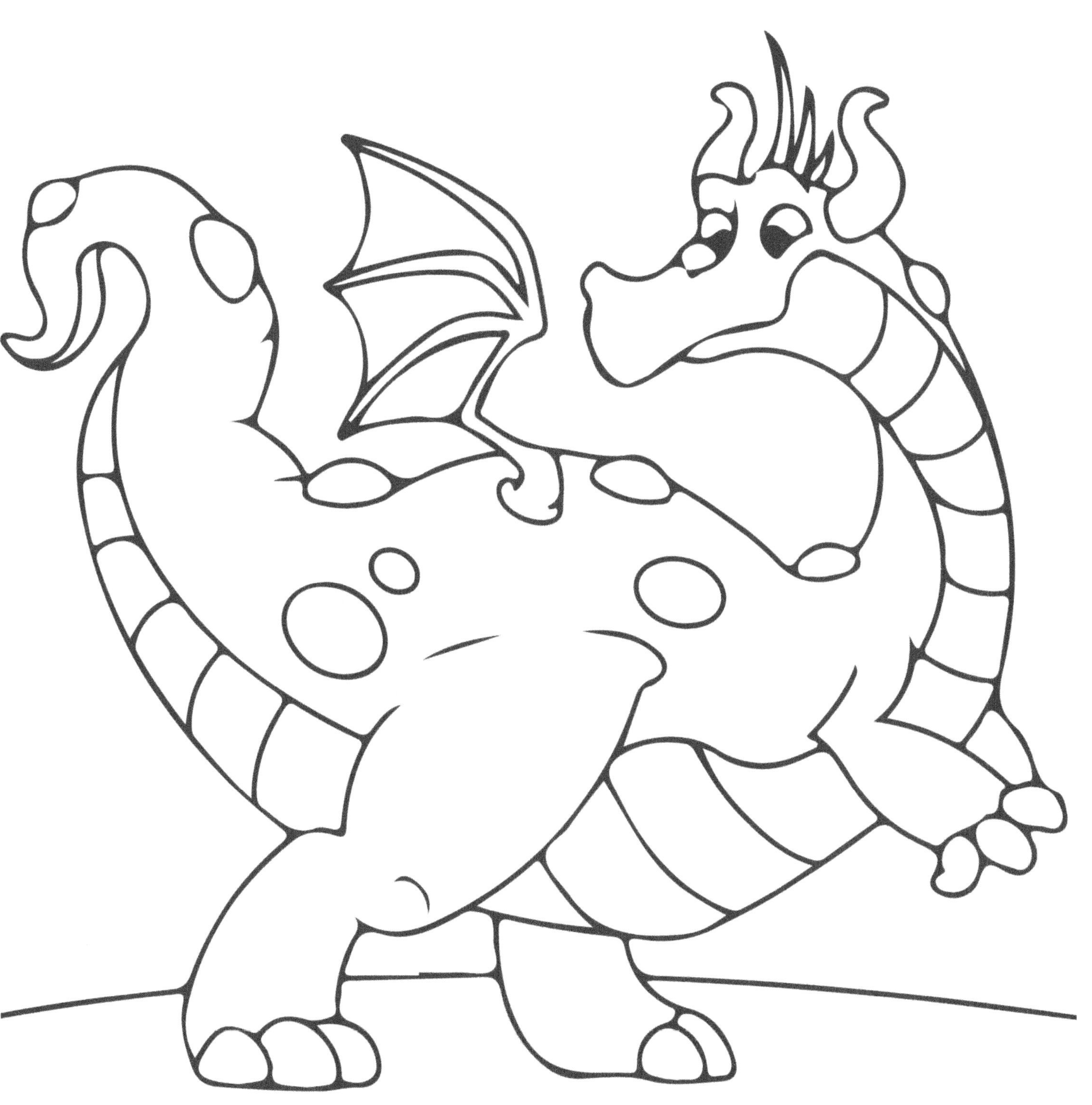

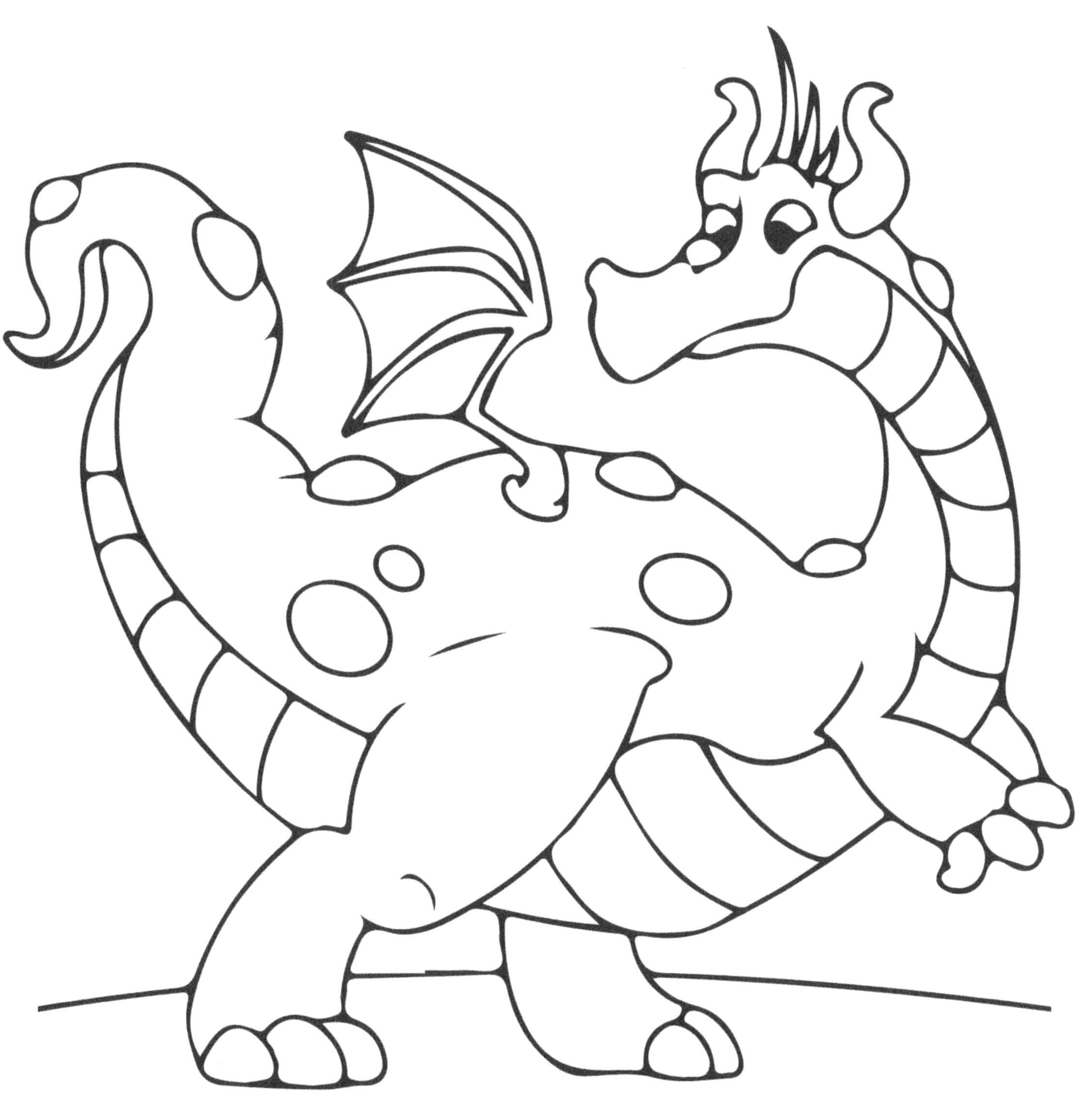

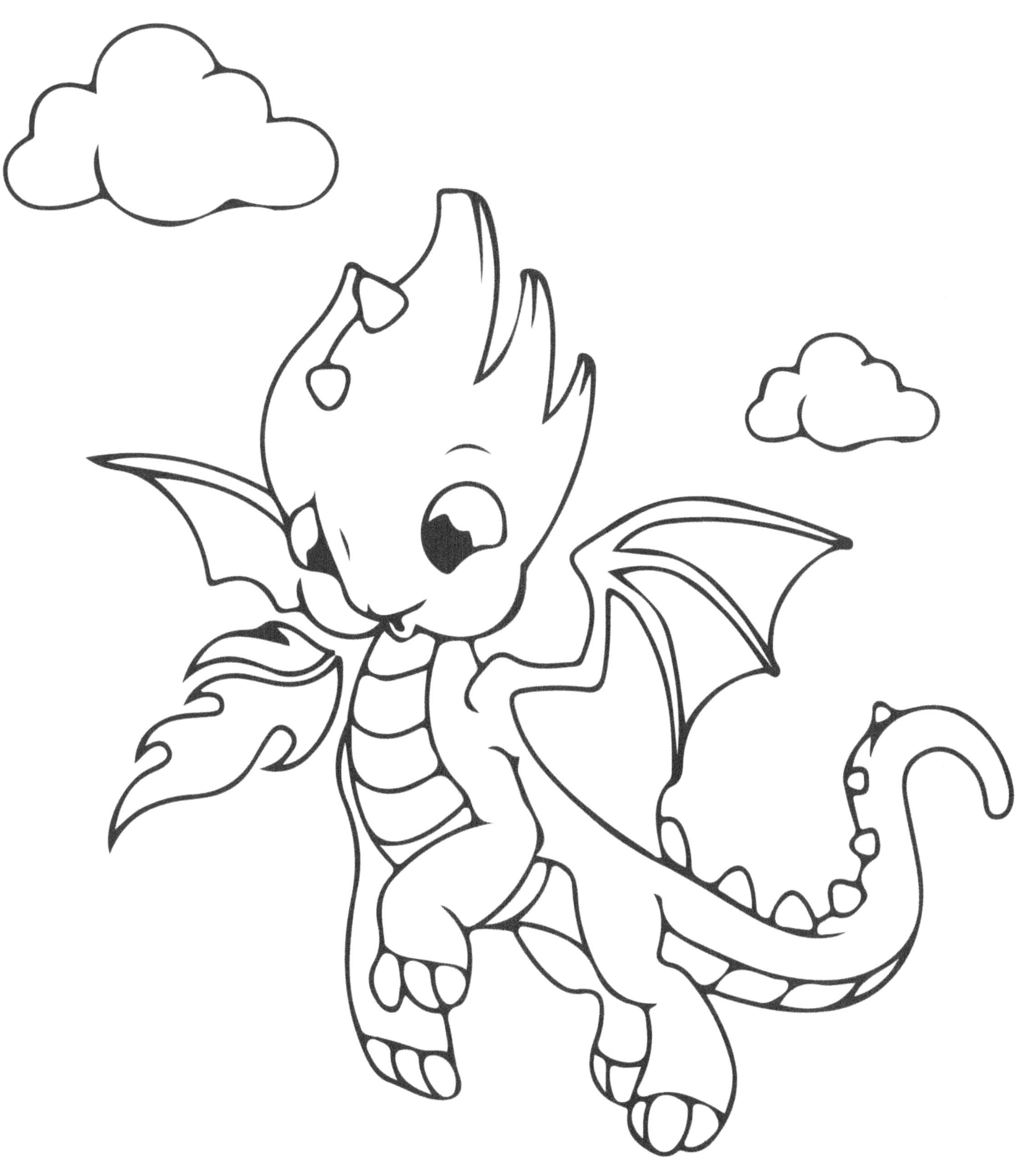

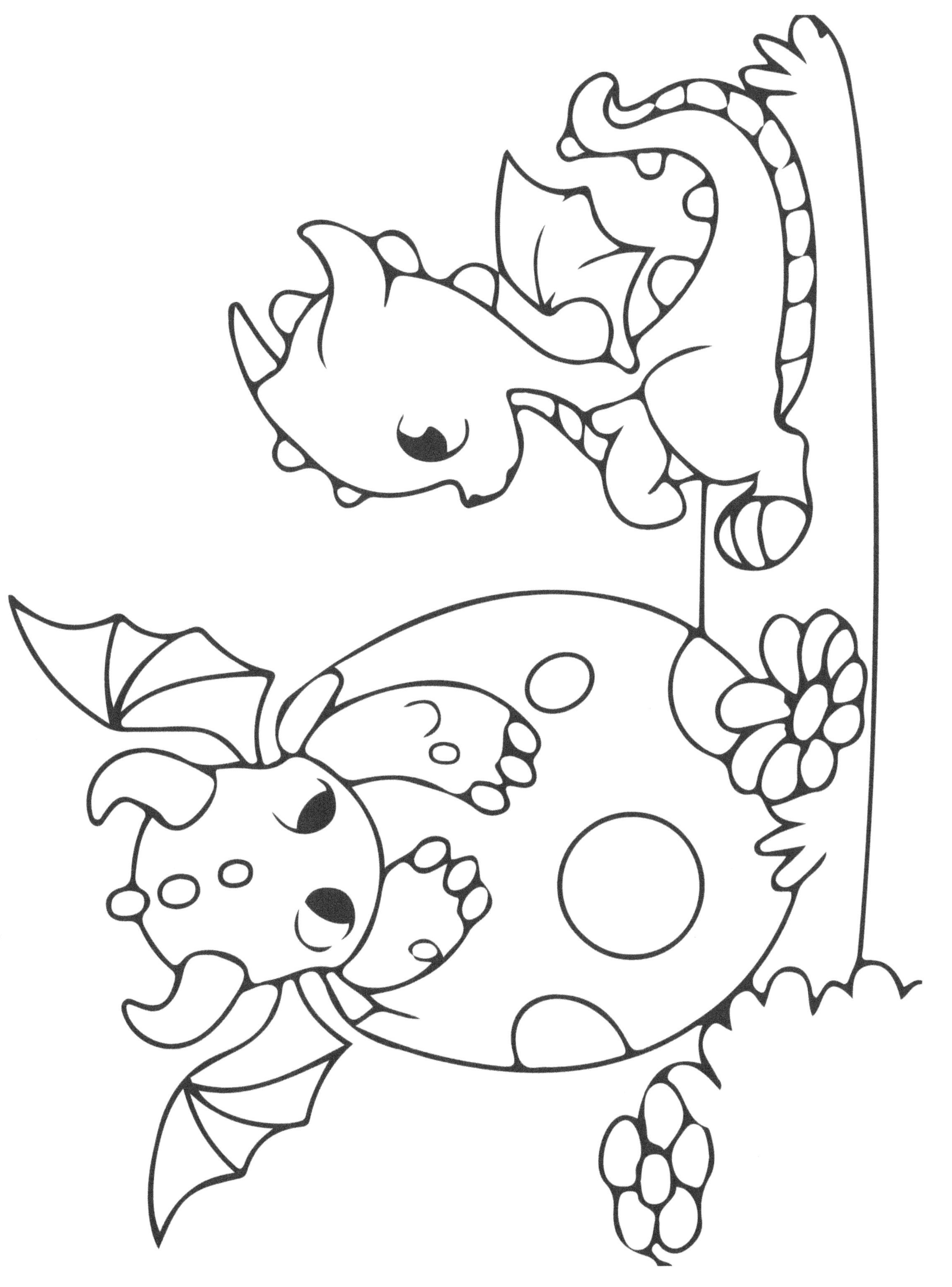

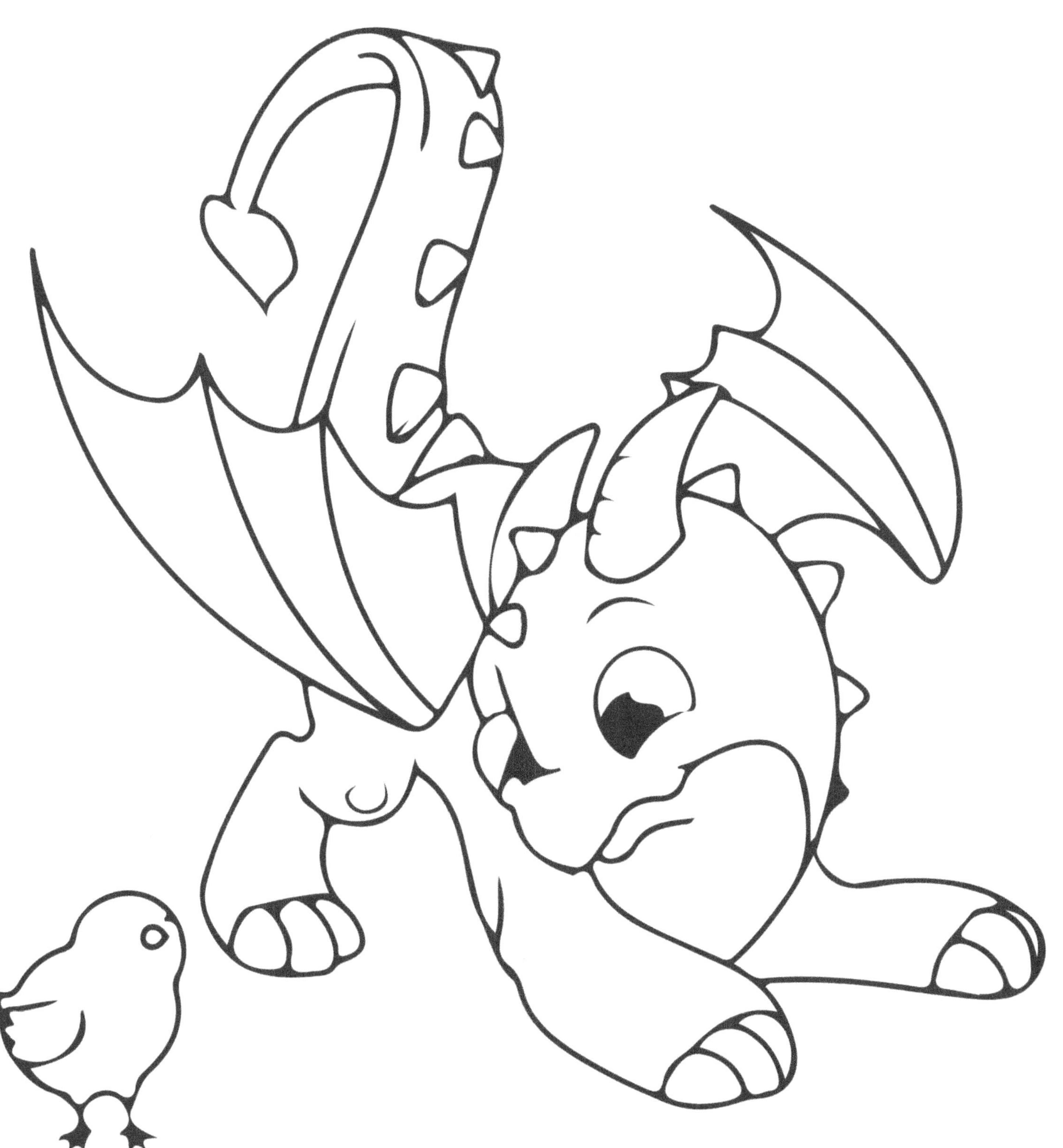

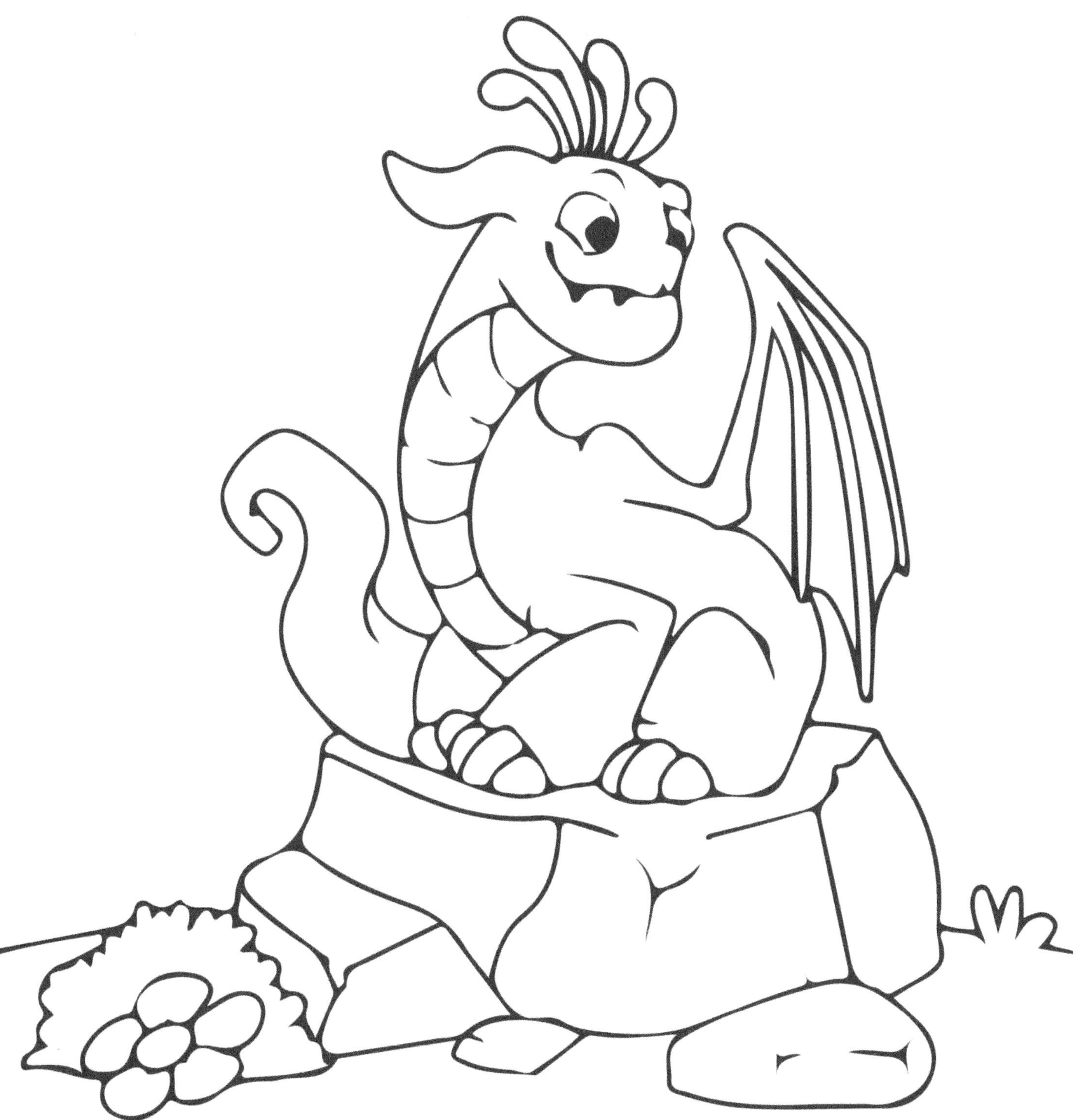

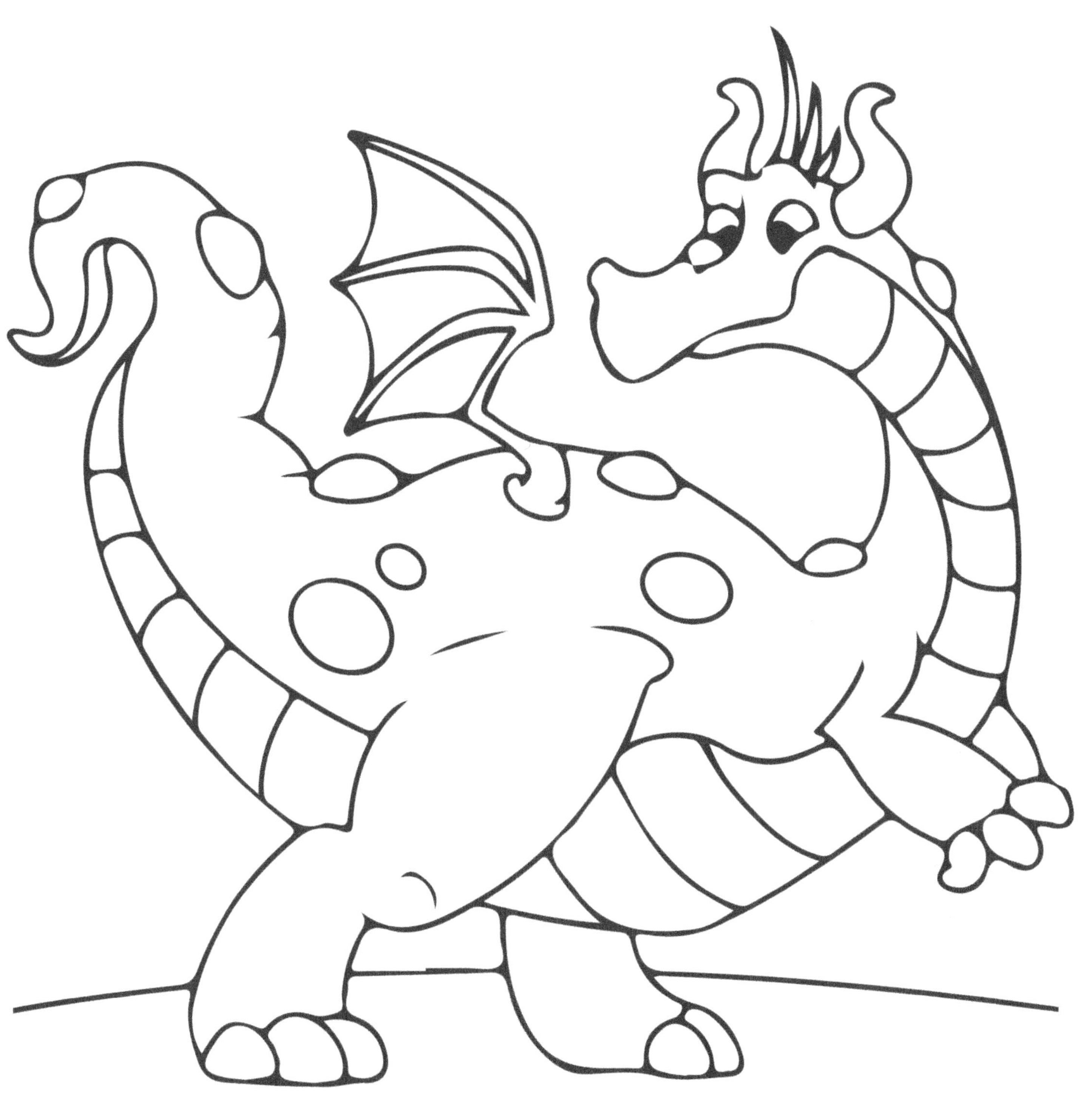

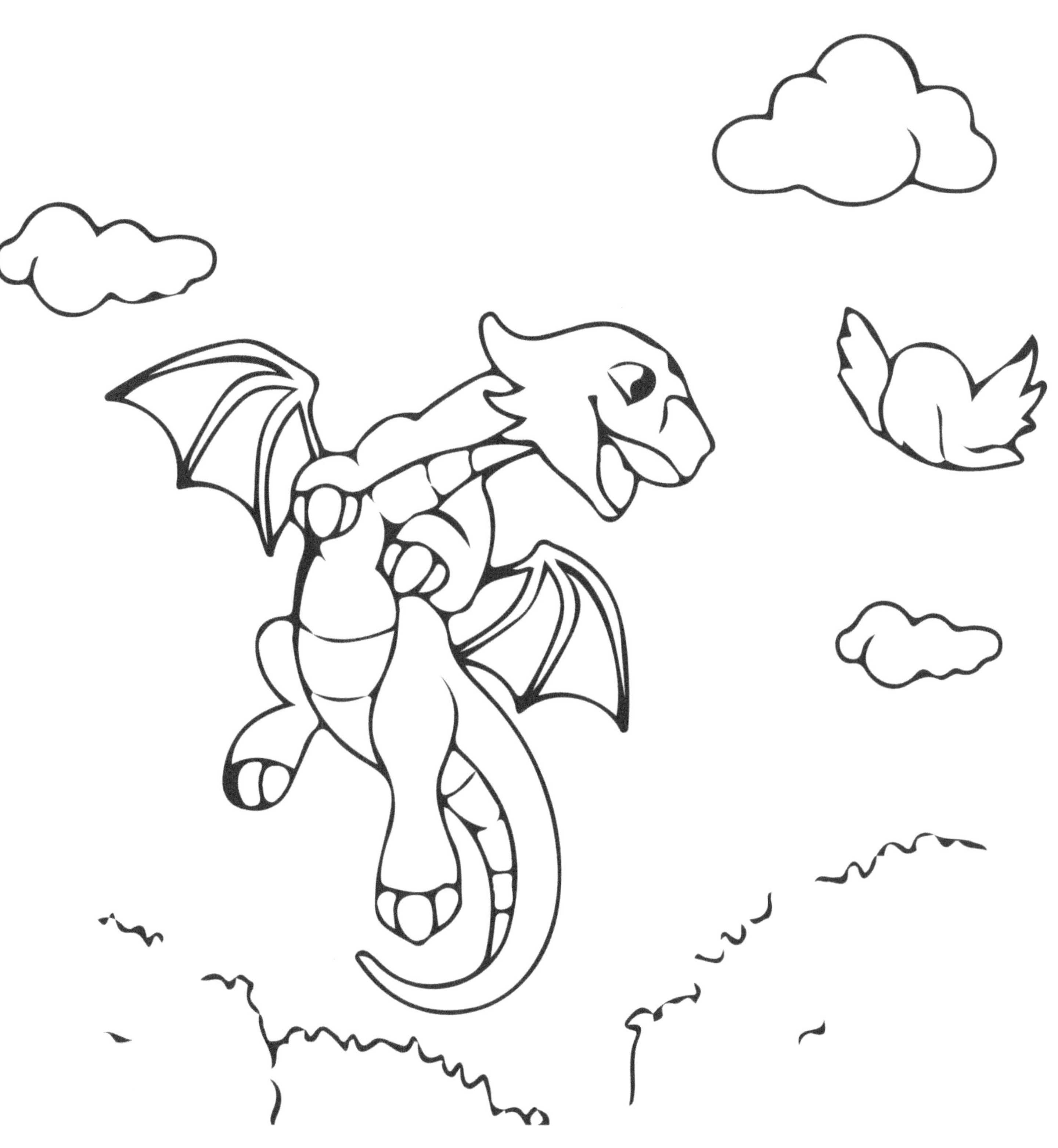

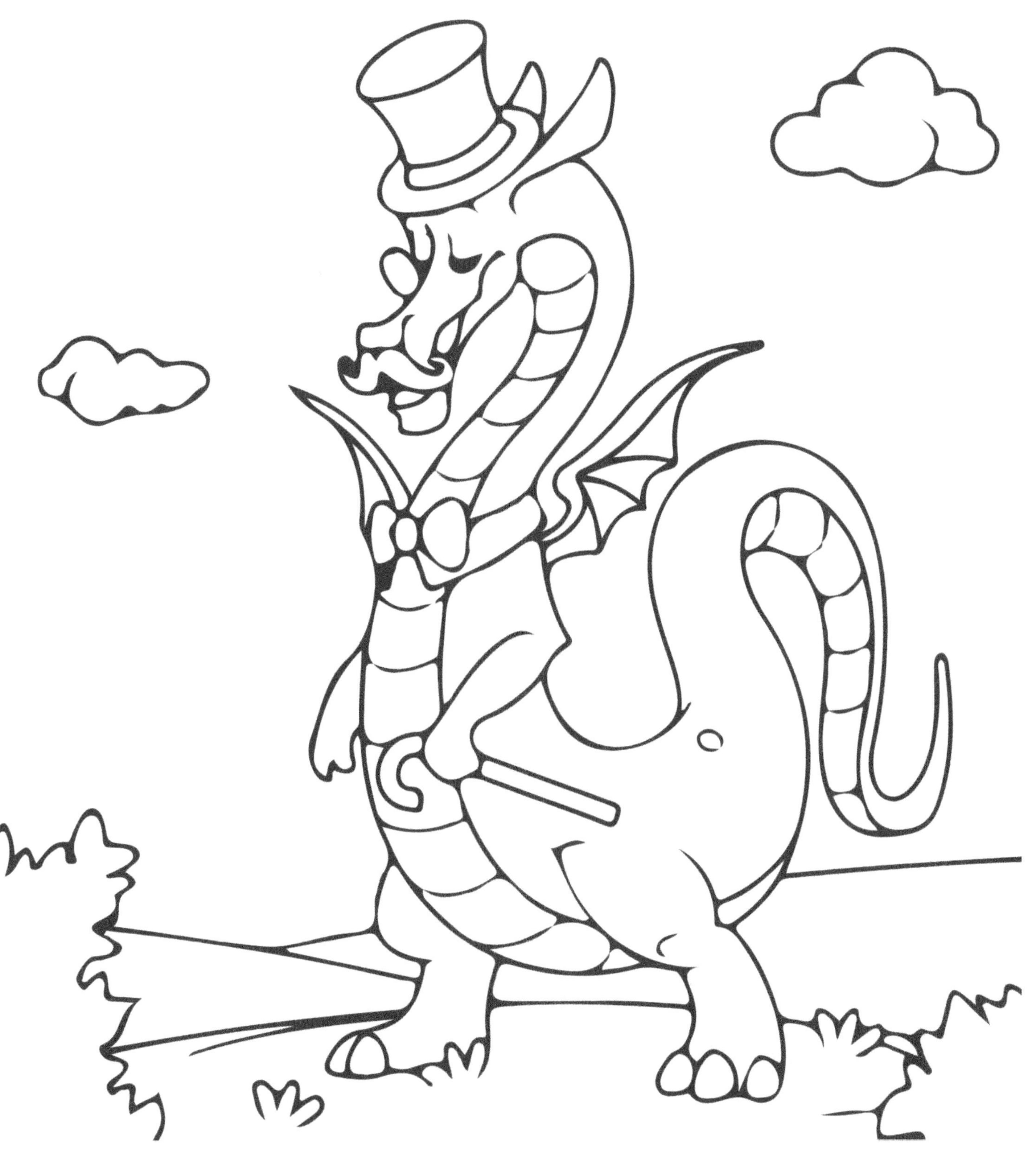

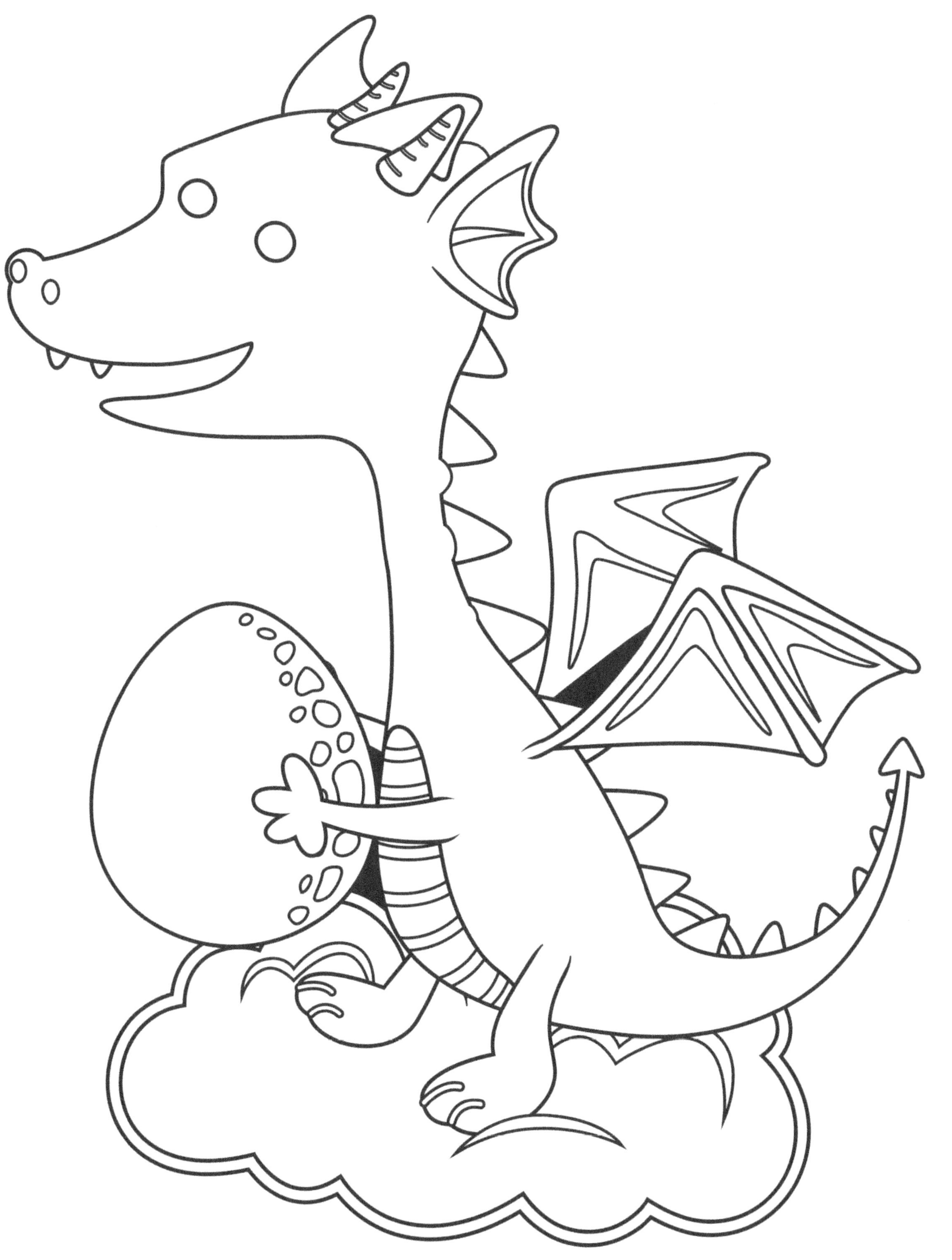

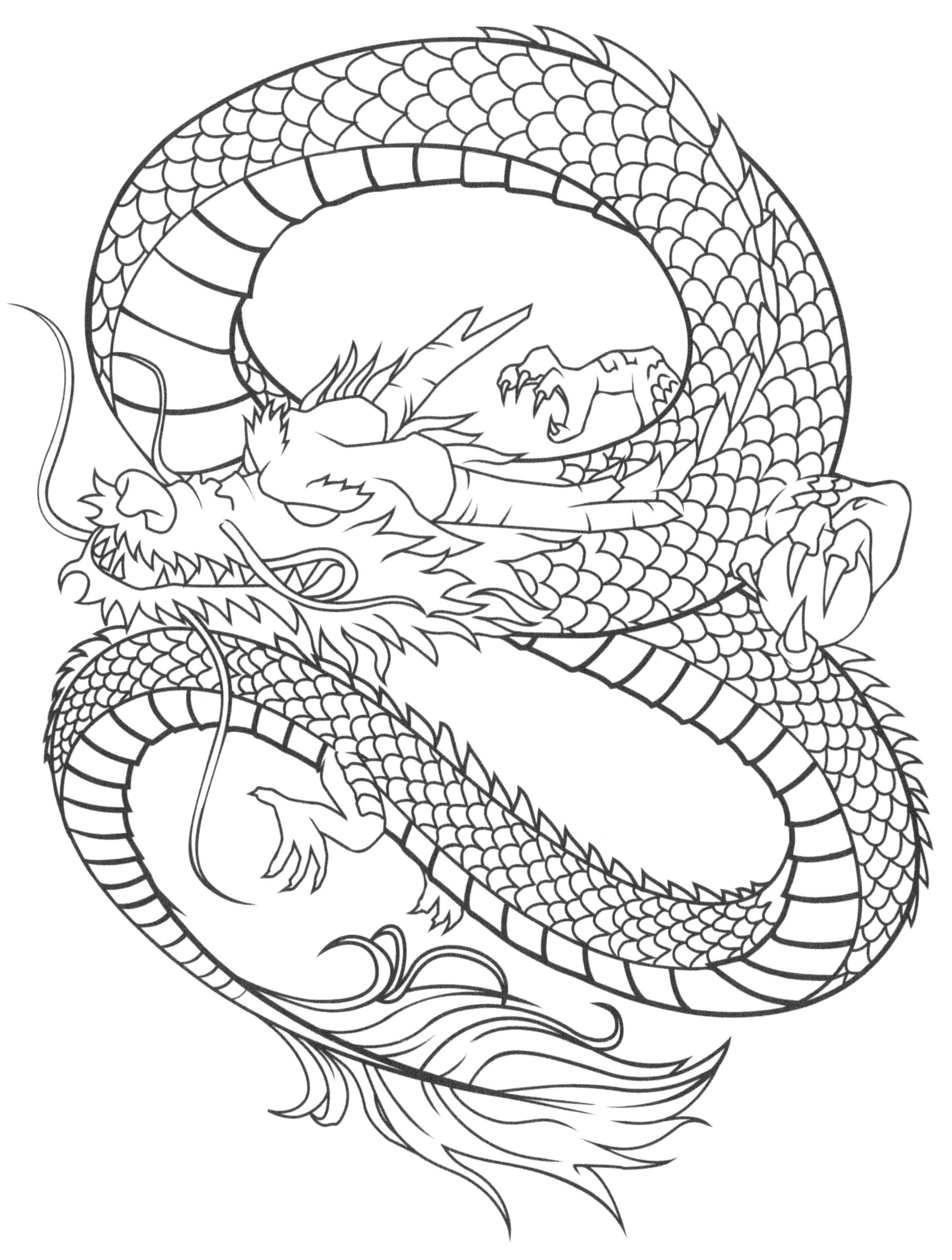

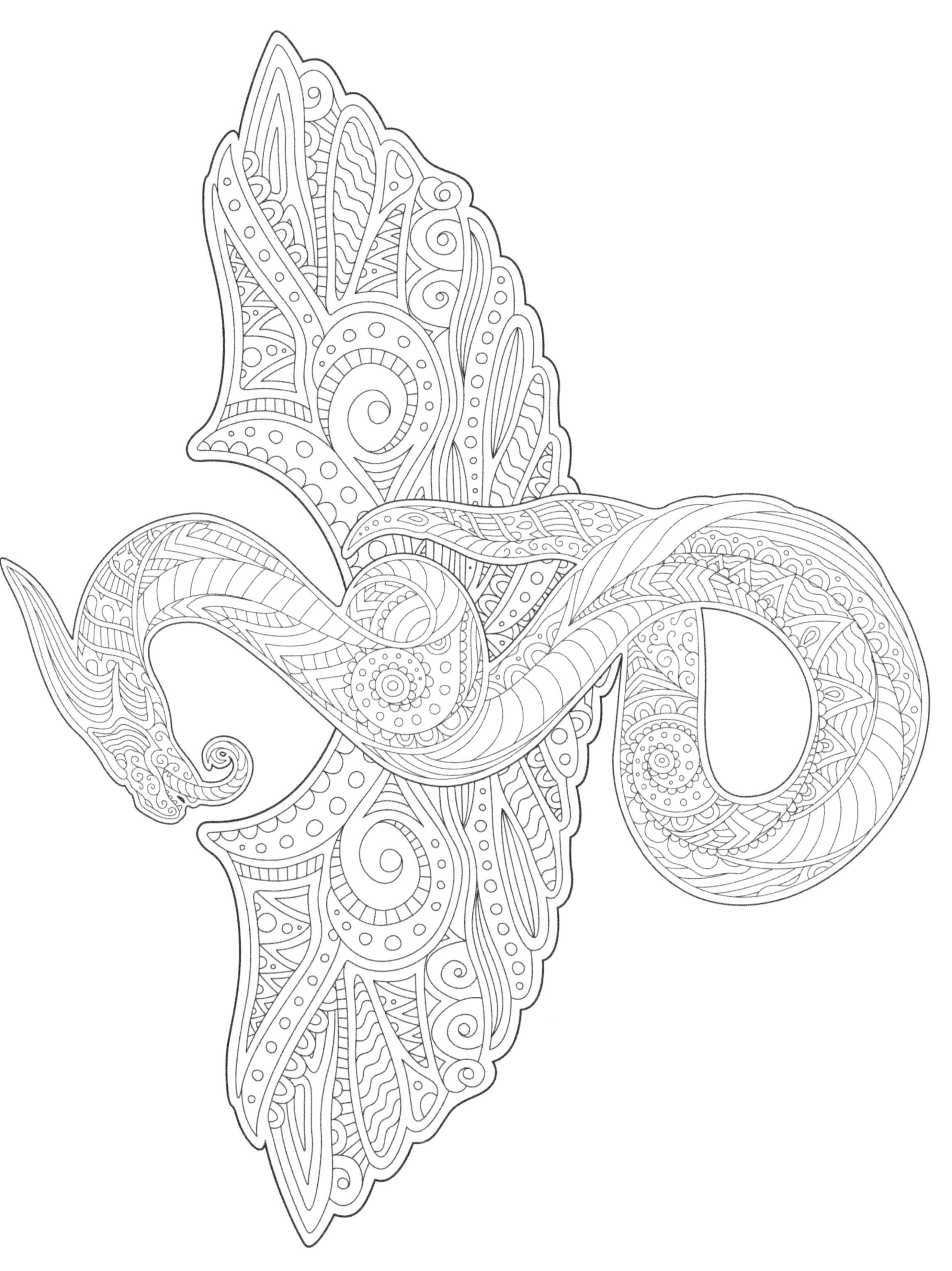

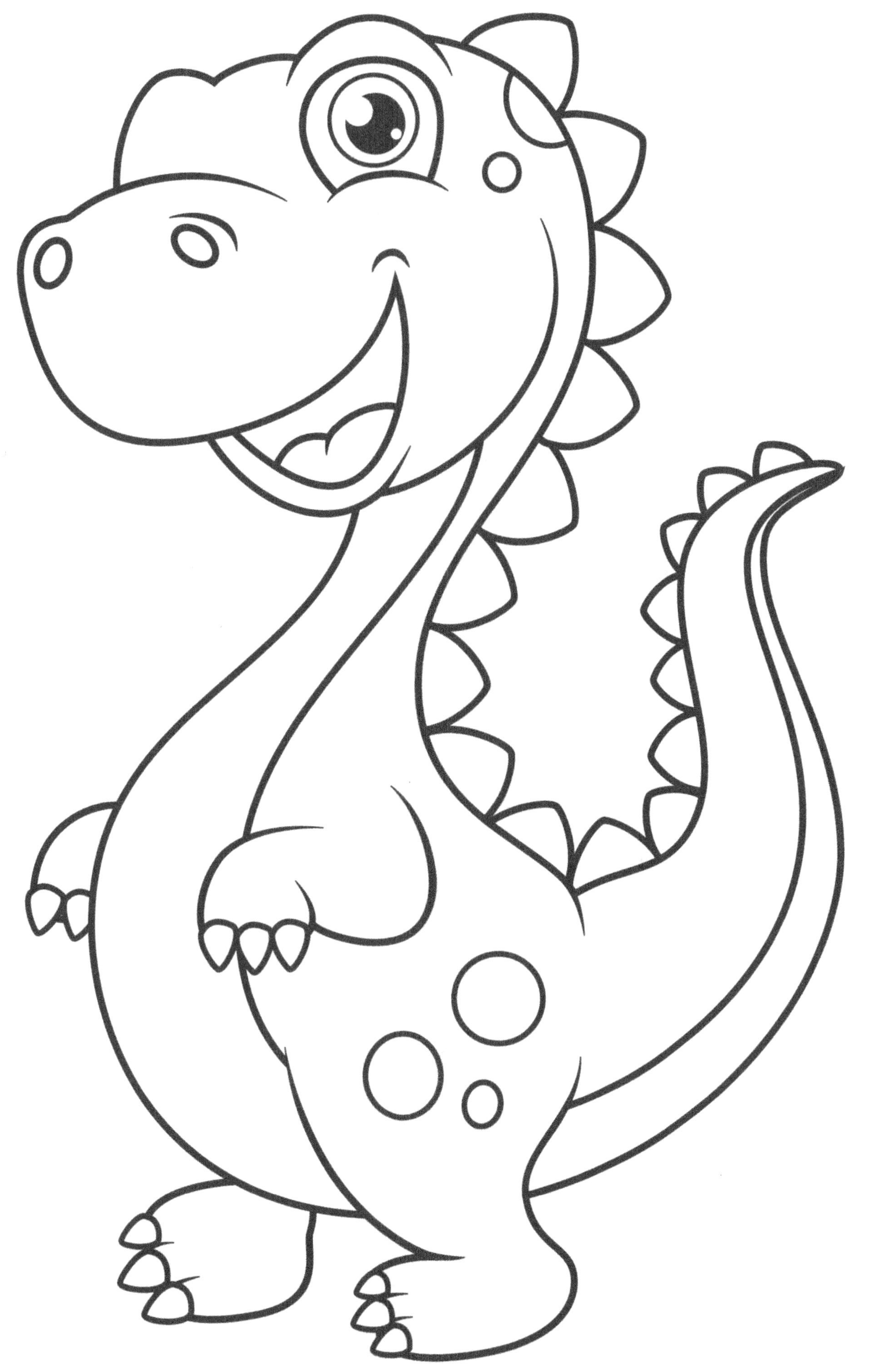

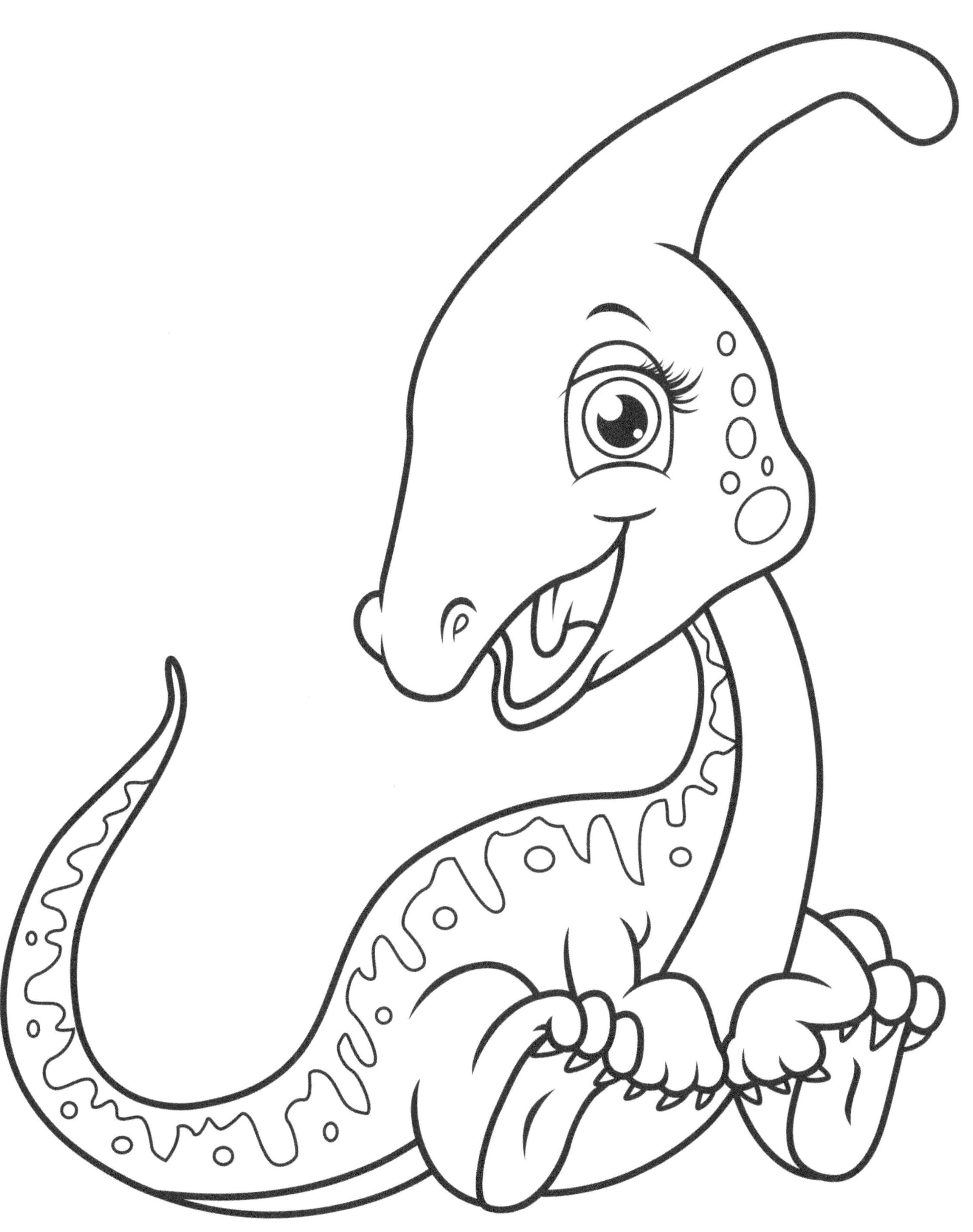

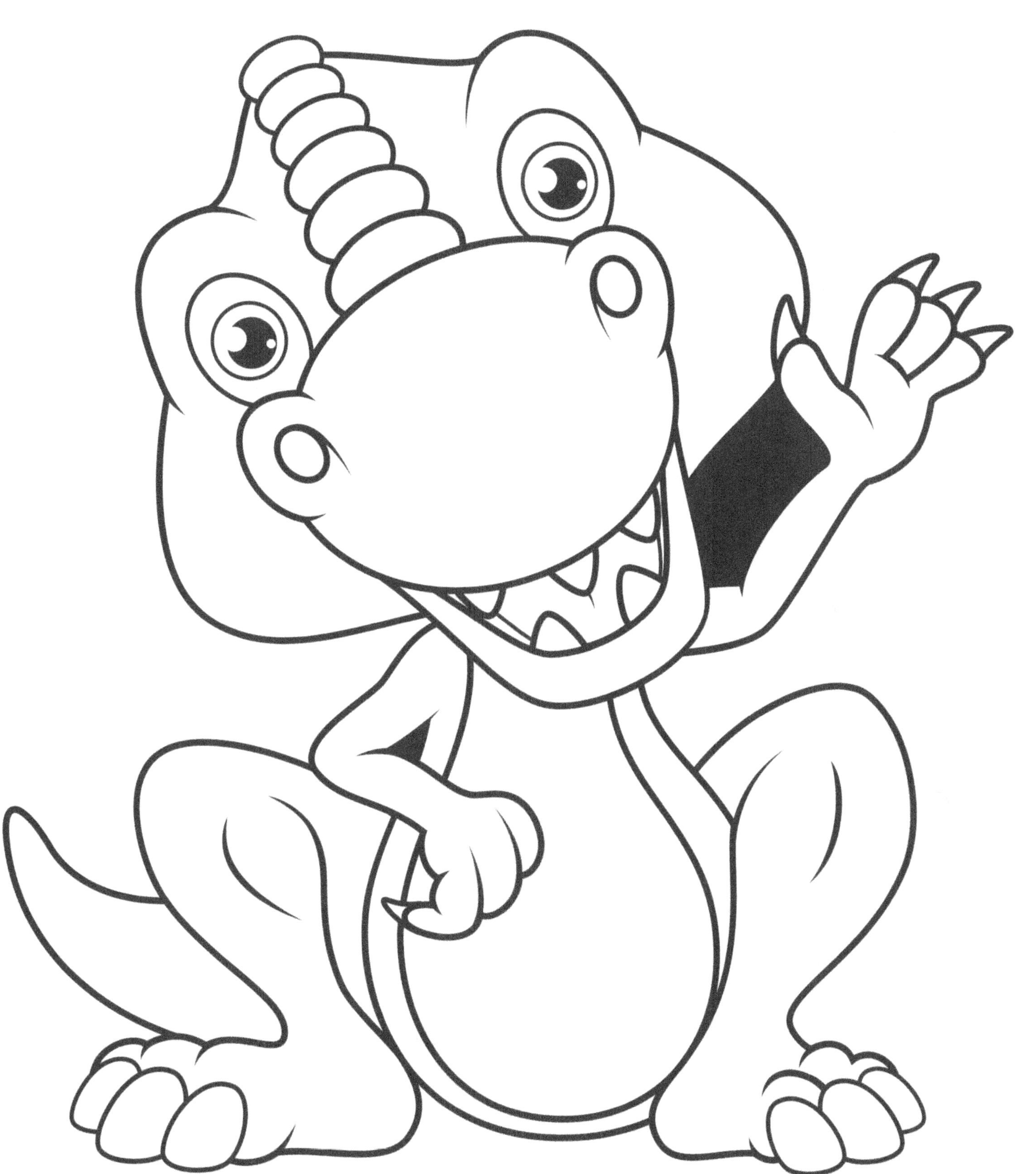